AWESOME FACTS
·FOR·
CURIOUS KIDS

8

·YEAR OLDS·

Illustrated by
Andrew Pinder

Written by Steve Martin
Edited by Lara Murphy
Designed by Derrian Bradder
Cover Design by John Bigwood

With special thanks to
Helen Cumberbatch

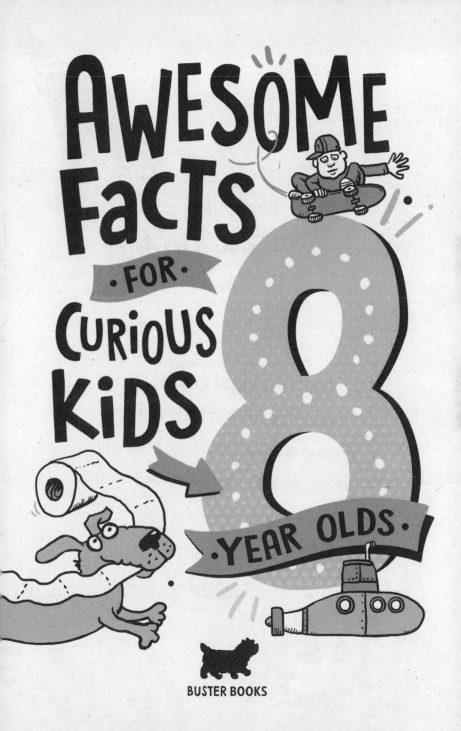

AWESOME FACTS

·FOR·
CURIOUS KIDS

8
·YEAR OLDS·

BUSTER BOOKS

First published in Great Britain in 2023 by Buster Books,
an imprint of Michael O'Mara Books Limited,
9 Lion Yard, Tremadoc Road, London SW4 7NQ

W www.mombooks.com/buster

f Buster Books

🐦 @BusterBooks

📷 @buster_books

A CIP catalogue record for this book is available from the British Library.

ISBN: 978-1-78055-927-8

1 3 5 7 9 10 8 6 4 2

This book was printed in February 2023 by
CPI Group (UK) Ltd, Croydon, CR0 4YY.

MIX
Paper | Supporting
responsible forestry
FSC® C171272

FSC
www.fsc.org

CONTENTS

Planet Earth   7

Human Body   21

History   33

Space   47

Animals   61

Sports   75

Technology   89

Underwater   103

Science   115

INTRODUCTION

Welcome to this totally awesome collection of mind-blowing facts for curious kids.

In this book you will learn about a sea animal with 3 hearts and 9 brains, a place where the Sun rises and sets just once a year, the snake that weighs the same as 10 eight-year-old children and a sport that's been played on the Moon.

★ giant rodents
   (page 68)

★ robot surgeons
   (page 102)

★ glowing insects
   (page 63)

★ exploding stars
   (page 48)

★ alien hunters
   (page 56)

★ floating trains
   (page 118)

Get ready to dive in and discover all these incredible things and more!

CHAPTER 1: PLANET EARTH

Port Royal was a pirate city in Jamaica and the richest place in the Americas. In 1692, it was completely destroyed by a powerful earthquake.

TA-RA, CAPTAIN MEANGUTS! IT'S EVERY PIRATE AND PARROT FOR HIMSELF, NOW!

PARDON ME!

Earthquakes happen when huge amounts of rock move underground. Their power is measured from 0 to 10 on the Richter scale. The strongest earthquake recorded was in Chile in 1960 and measured 9.5.

Tornadoes are funnel-shaped swirling winds. In the bottom half of the world (below the equator), they usually spin in a clockwise direction and in the top half they spin anticlockwise.

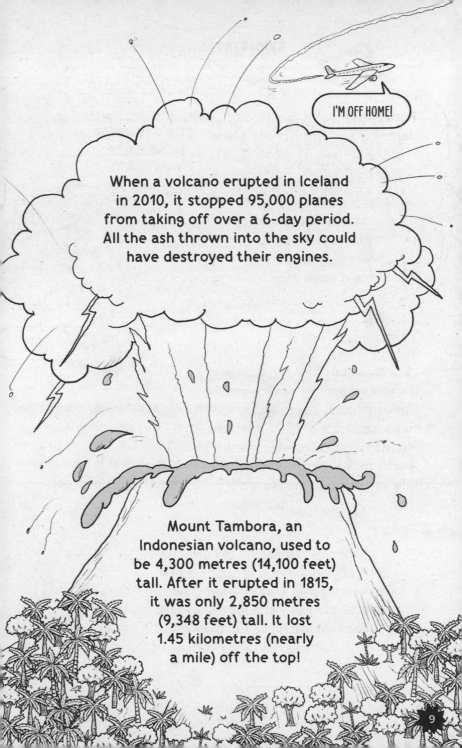

I'M OFF HOME!

When a volcano erupted in Iceland in 2010, it stopped 95,000 planes from taking off over a 6-day period. All the ash thrown into the sky could have destroyed their engines.

Mount Tambora, an Indonesian volcano, used to be 4,300 metres (14,100 feet) tall. After it erupted in 1815, it was only 2,850 metres (9,348 feet) tall. It lost 1.45 kilometres (nearly a mile) off the top!

Rainforests

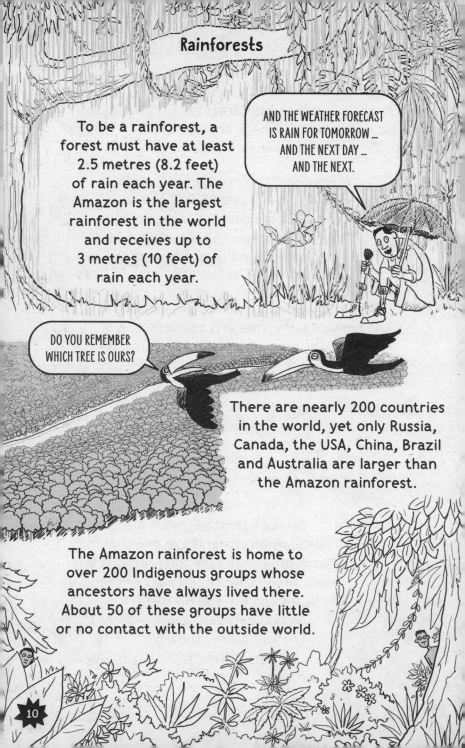

To be a rainforest, a forest must have at least 2.5 metres (8.2 feet) of rain each year. The Amazon is the largest rainforest in the world and receives up to 3 metres (10 feet) of rain each year.

AND THE WEATHER FORECAST IS RAIN FOR TOMORROW ... AND THE NEXT DAY ... AND THE NEXT.

DO YOU REMEMBER WHICH TREE IS OURS?

There are nearly 200 countries in the world, yet only Russia, Canada, the USA, China, Brazil and Australia are larger than the Amazon rainforest.

The Amazon rainforest is home to over 200 Indigenous groups whose ancestors have always lived there. About 50 of these groups have little or no contact with the outside world.

Estimated at 130–180 million years old, Australia's Daintree rainforest is the oldest in the world, where unique animals such as the tree kangaroo live.

The Congo Basin rainforest in Africa is the world's second largest rainforest. It is home to elephants, gorillas, chimpanzees, buffaloes, bonobos and many other species.

HEY!

Rainforests don't have to be in hot places. Besides tropical rainforests, there are cooler temperate rainforests. The Tongass rainforest in Alaska is a temperate rainforest, where bears, moose and wolves live.

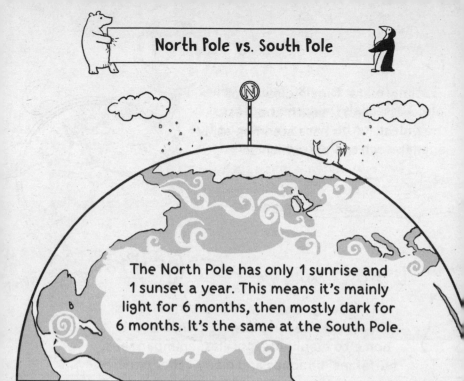

The North Pole has only 1 sunrise and 1 sunset a year. This means it's mainly light for 6 months, then mostly dark for 6 months. It's the same at the South Pole.

The North Pole is at sea level but the South Pole is 2,835 metres (9,300 feet) higher. This is one reason the South Pole is colder.

Explorers arrived at the North Pole in 1909, and the South Pole over 2 and a half years later in 1911.

RIGHT! THAT'S THE NORTH AND SOUTH POLES DONE. WHERE NEXT?

There are 4 main directions – north, east, south and west. Weirdly, if you are standing at the North Pole, whichever direction you walk in is south. If you are at the South Pole, every direction is north.

At the South Pole, the ice is a whopping 2,700 metres (8,860 feet) thick. At the North Pole, it's only up to 3 metres (10 feet) thick.

No country owns the North or South Poles.

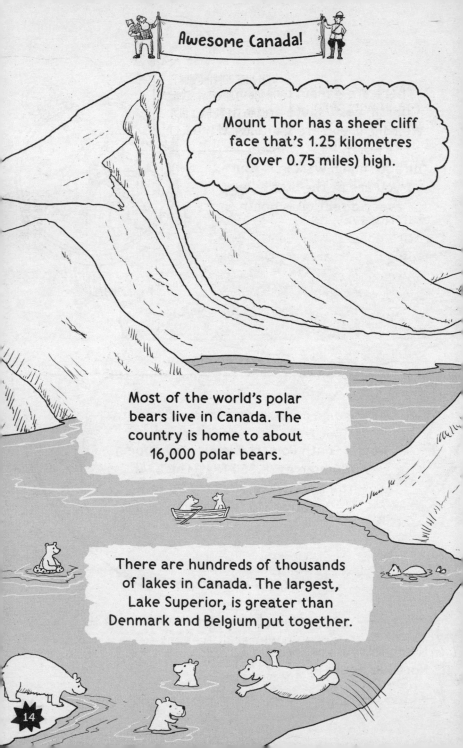

Mount Thor has a sheer cliff face that's 1.25 kilometres (over 0.75 miles) high.

Most of the world's polar bears live in Canada. The country is home to about 16,000 polar bears.

There are hundreds of thousands of lakes in Canada. The largest, Lake Superior, is greater than Denmark and Belgium put together.

Nunavut is a large area in northern Canada where the Inuit people live. Although only 13 countries in the world are bigger than Nunavut, its entire population would fit into an average-sized soccer stadium.

I'M JUST POPPING NEXT DOOR TO BORROW SOME SUGAR. I'LL BE BACK IN A COUPLE OF WEEKS.

The border between Canada and the USA is 8,891 kilometres (5,525 miles) long. If a border guard marched along it for 8 hours every day, it would take over 7.5 months to get from one end to the other.

Ottawa, Canada's capital, has a canal measuring 7.8 kilometres (4.8 miles) long. In winter, it freezes over and everyone gets their skates on.

15

Planet Earth's People

The equator is an imaginary line around the middle of the Earth. The top half of the world is the busiest, with almost 9 out of every 10 people living there.

Almost 1 person in every 5 lives in China.

Just over 4 people are born every second!

I ONLY TURNED MY BACK FOR A MOMENT!

Every year, there are over
65 million more people
on the planet.

The world is divided into 7 continents: Europe (1), Asia (2),
Africa (3), North America (4), South America (5), Australia
(6) and Antarctica (7). More than half the world's population
live in Asia. No one has a permanent home in Antarctica.

More than half of the people in the
world live in towns and cities, and the
numbers are increasing all the time.

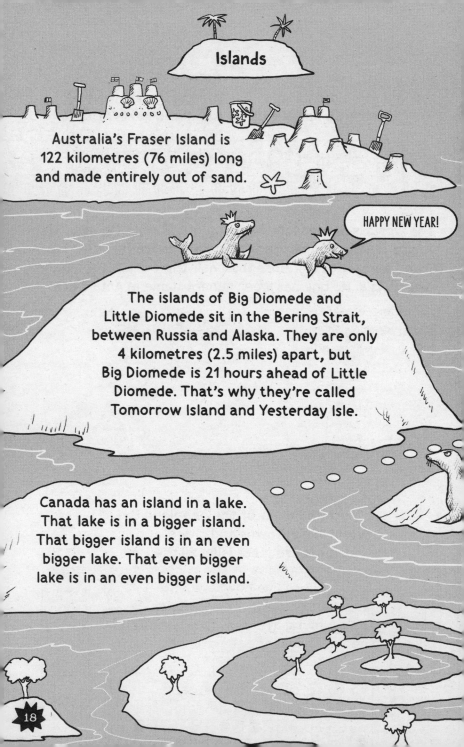

Islands

Australia's Fraser Island is 122 kilometres (76 miles) long and made entirely out of sand.

HAPPY NEW YEAR!

The islands of Big Diomede and Little Diomede sit in the Bering Strait, between Russia and Alaska. They are only 4 kilometres (2.5 miles) apart, but Big Diomede is 21 hours ahead of Little Diomede. That's why they're called Tomorrow Island and Yesterday Isle.

Canada has an island in a lake. That lake is in a bigger island. That bigger island is in an even bigger lake. That even bigger lake is in an even bigger island.

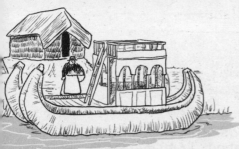

Up to 4,000 people are said to live on floating islands on Lake Titicaca in South America. The islands are made out of roots and reeds.

CABIN, PREPARE FOR LANDING ...

WE HAVEN'T EVEN TAKEN OFF YET!

You can take a plane from Papa Westray to Westray in Scotland. The 2 islands are less than 3 kilometres (just over 1.5 miles) apart and the flight takes no more than 90 seconds.

The island of Madagascar is about 400 kilometres (250 miles) off the coast of Africa. Many of the animals there live nowhere else in the world. This includes lemurs, aye-ayes (a type of monkey) and tomato frogs.

NICE TO MEET YOU!

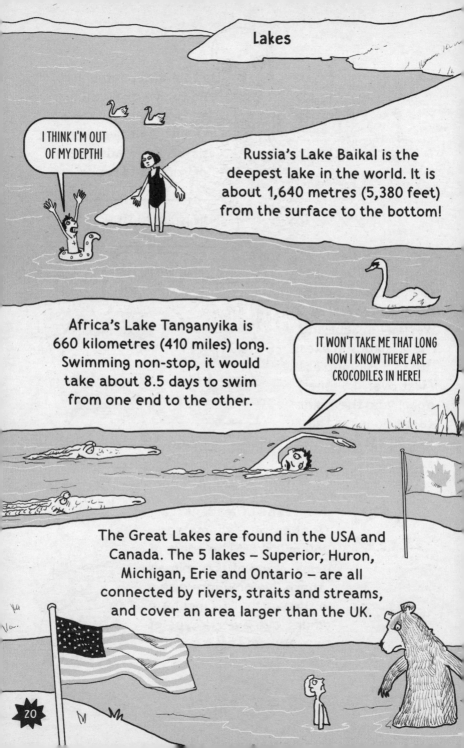

CHAPTER 2:
HUMAN
BODY

Gross Facts

Your feet have 250,000 sweat glands, which make about 300 millilitres (0.6 pints) of sweat every day. That's a whole glassful!

In a single day, a person's mouth makes enough spit to fill at least 2 cans of soda.

Each person uses about 100 toilet rolls in a year.

People swallow up to 2 litres (about 4.2 pints) of snot every day. That's about 6 glasses.

Everyone farts up to 15 times a day – enough to fill a balloon!

ACHOO! ANYONE FOR A NICE, REFRESHING GLASS OF SNOT?

Blood

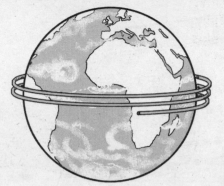

The tubes carrying blood around your body are called veins, arteries and capillaries. You have enough of these to wrap around the Earth almost 2.5 times!

The heart pumps about 5 litres (10.5 pints) of blood around the body every minute.

The human body contains just over 5.5 litres (11.6 pints) of blood. That's about 20 full glasses.

Blood contains a teeny-tiny amount of iron. This is really important because iron helps the blood carry oxygen around the body.

To stop a nosebleed, don't lean back! The trick is to lean forward, pinch your nose (to trap the blood there) and wait for it to stop.

DO YOU FANCY A SWIM?

ER ... NO, THANKS!

Every year, people give about 57 million litres (over 120 million pints) of blood to help people who need it. That's enough to fill 23 enormous Olympic-size swimming pools.

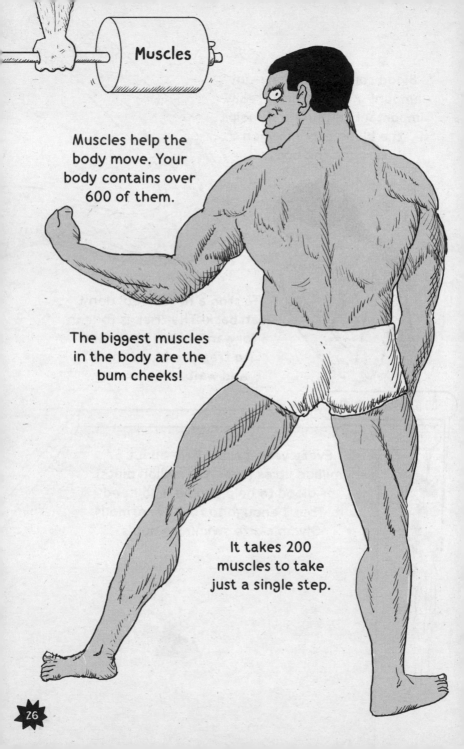

Muscles

Muscles help the body move. Your body contains over 600 of them.

The biggest muscles in the body are the bum cheeks!

It takes 200 muscles to take just a single step.

The strongest muscles
are on each side of
the mouth and are
used for chewing.

Muscles are everywhere.
Even the tongue and
heart are muscles, and
are commonly described
as 'muscular organs'.

Muscles make up
over a third of the
body's weight.

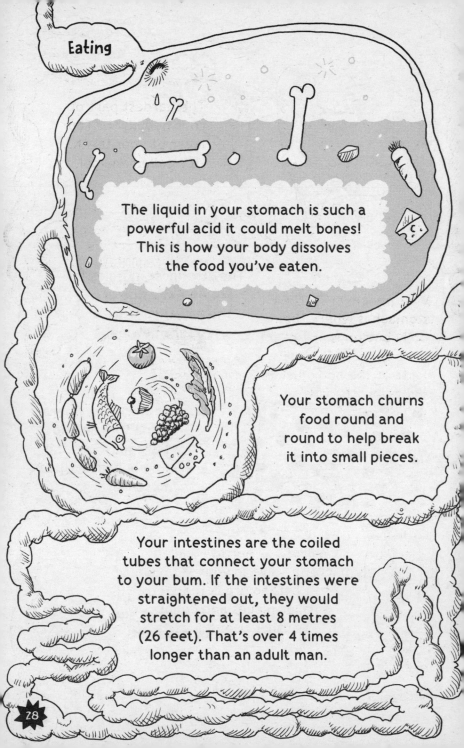

The liquid in your stomach is such a powerful acid it could melt bones! This is how your body dissolves the food you've eaten.

Your stomach churns food round and round to help break it into small pieces.

Your intestines are the coiled tubes that connect your stomach to your bum. If the intestines were straightened out, they would stretch for at least 8 metres (26 feet). That's over 4 times longer than an adult man.

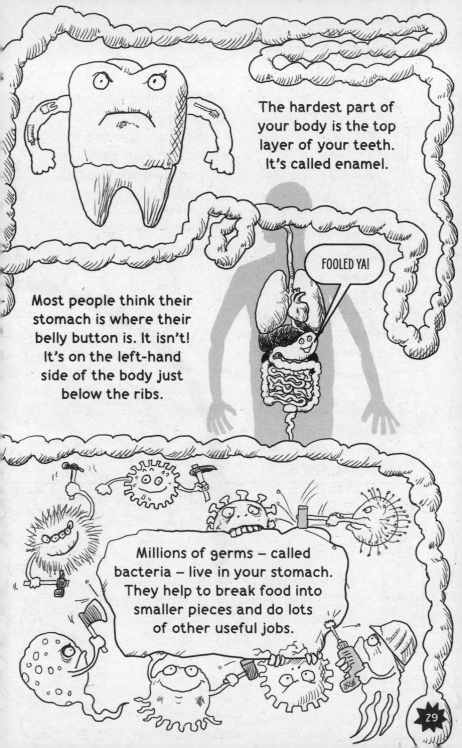

The hardest part of your body is the top layer of your teeth. It's called enamel.

FOOLED YA!

Most people think their stomach is where their belly button is. It isn't! It's on the left-hand side of the body just below the ribs.

Millions of germs – called bacteria – live in your stomach. They help to break food into smaller pieces and do lots of other useful jobs.

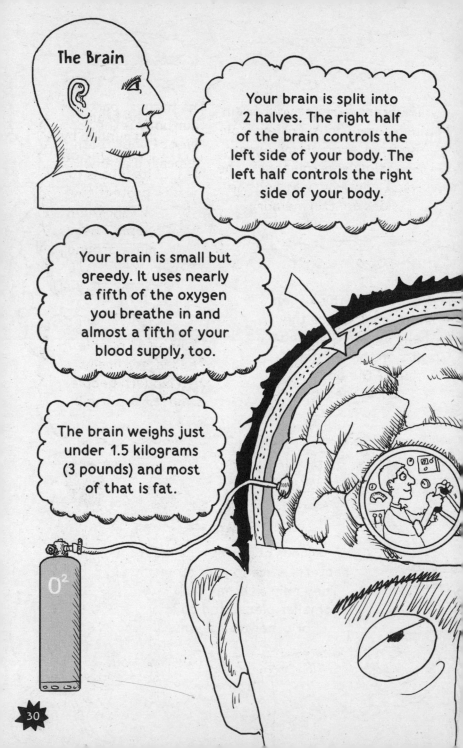

The Brain

Your brain is split into 2 halves. The right half of the brain controls the left side of your body. The left half controls the right side of your body.

Your brain is small but greedy. It uses nearly a fifth of the oxygen you breathe in and almost a fifth of your blood supply, too.

The brain weighs just under 1.5 kilograms (3 pounds) and most of that is fat.

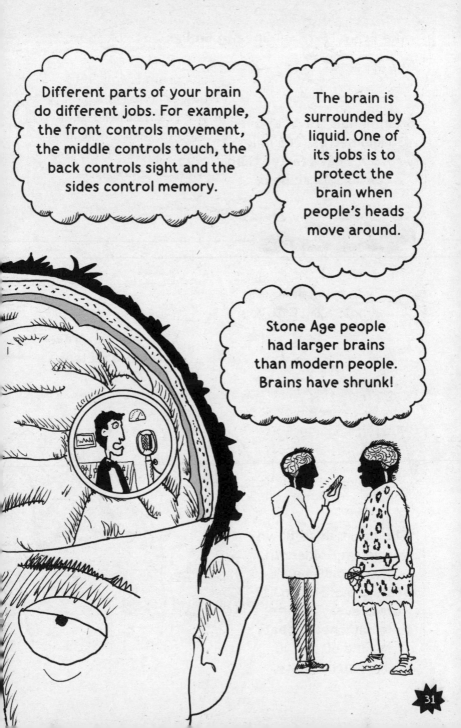

Different parts of your brain do different jobs. For example, the front controls movement, the middle controls touch, the back controls sight and the sides control memory.

The brain is surrounded by liquid. One of its jobs is to protect the brain when people's heads move around.

Stone Age people had larger brains than modern people. Brains have shrunk!

Speedy Bodies

Brain signals travel at over 430 kilometres (268 miles) per hour. That's faster than a Formula 1 racing car.

I NEED TO GO FASTER IF I'M GOING TO CATCH UP WITH MY THOUGHTS.

A sneeze can travel about 8 metres (27 feet).

The heart slows down as you get older. An 8-year-old's heart beats around 70 to 110 times every minute. An adult's heart beats around 60 to 100 times per minute.

CHAPTER 3:
HISTORY

Battles

In 1066, the Battle of Hastings was fought between an army from France and an English army. The battle was later recorded through scenes sewn on to a huge piece of cloth called the Bayeux Tapestry.

SLOW DOWN! I CAN'T SEW THAT FAST.

TURN IT AROUND!

In 202 BCE, a famous general, Hannibal, tried to defeat the Romans with his war elephants. It didn't work. When the elephants charged, the Romans just stepped aside and let them run past.

BYE...

A 'civil war' is when a country fights itself. This happened in the USA in the 1860s. The most famous battle was at Gettysburg, where the army from the North defeated the army from the South.

The Battle of Britain took place in the sky. During the Second World War (1939–1945), British pilots spent nearly 4 months fighting off the German air force.

Over 2 million Russian and German soldiers took part in the Battle of Stalingrad in the Second World War. As so many people were involved, some historians call Stalingrad the biggest battle of all time.

Over 2,000 years ago, 3 well-trained, heavily armed Roman legions marched into battle in the dark Teutoburg Forest in Germany ... Most of the 20,000 soldiers were never seen again.

HELLO, ANYONE IN THERE?

Famous People

Cleopatra, who ruled Egypt over 2,000 years ago, certainly knew how to make an entrance. On one occasion, the famous queen dressed as a Greek goddess and sailed into the city of Tarsus sitting in a golden boat with silver oars.

Leonardo da Vinci is one of the most famous artists of all time. He painted the *Mona Lisa* over 500 years ago.

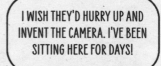

I WISH THEY'D HURRY UP AND INVENT THE CAMERA. I'VE BEEN SITTING HERE FOR DAYS!

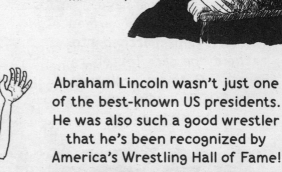

Abraham Lincoln wasn't just one of the best-known US presidents. He was also such a good wrestler that he's been recognized by America's Wrestling Hall of Fame!

A lot of Roman emperors weren't very nice, and Nero was especially cruel. Legend says that he played his lute while the city of Rome burned to the ground.

Marie Curie lived at a time when people said women couldn't be scientists. She didn't listen and won the Nobel Prize (the biggest prize in science) twice ... and her daughter won 1 as well.

Shigeru Miyamoto is considered the most famous video games designer ever. Without this genius, we wouldn't have Donkey Kong, Mario or Zelda!

Ancient Greece

Ancient Greece wasn't 1 kingdom. It was split into lots of city states. The most famous were Athens and Sparta.

The Greeks believed in lots of gods and goddesses. The most important 12 lived on Mount Olympus and their leader was called Zeus.

The Greeks were famous thinkers. Today, people still study the works of genius philosophers such as Plato and Aristotle.

Nobody knows if the famous Trojan War really happened. The Greek soldiers were said to have won the war by hiding some troops in a huge wooden horse that the Trojans pulled into their city, Troy. At night, the men secretly left the horse and opened the city gates to let the rest of their army in.

The Greeks built an incredible temple overlooking Athens. It's called the Parthenon and it's still there today – even though it was built 2,500 years ago.

Ancient Greeks invented theatre and the Olympic Games. They studied maths and medicine and gave us words such as 'gym' and 'academy'. Without the Greeks, the modern world would be very different.

Maya, Incas and Aztecs

The Maya people appeared in Central America (Mexico and countries near it) over 3,500 years ago. There are still Maya people living there today.

Maya children were named after the day they were born. Luckily, every day of the year had a different name.

HELLO MONDAY!
HELLO TUESDAY ...
AND WEDNESDAY ...
AND THURSDAY ...

The Aztec people lived in Mexico. Their empire lasted for almost 200 years until they were defeated by the Spanish in 1521.

According to legend, the Aztec city of Tenochtitlán was founded on the spot where an eagle was seen eating a snake while perched on a cactus. The historic centre of Mexico City stands in the same place today.

The Incas lived high in the Andes Mountains in South America. Their huge empire stretched for about 4,000 kilometres (2,500 miles).

The most famous Inca ruin is the city of Machu Picchu. It lies high up in the Andes Mountains at a height of around 2,430 metres (7,972 feet) and is Peru's most popular tourist attraction.

Chinese alchemists invented gunpowder long before anyone else. They didn't just use it for fireworks, though. Their armies used it for bombs, rockets and cannons.

I THINK YOU NEED A BIGGER BOW.

Longbows were around 1.8 metres (6 feet) tall – as tall as the archers firing them! They helped about 6,000 English soldiers defeat at least twice as many French troops at the Battle of Agincourt in 1415.

The mace was a simple but horrible weapon. This club had a big metal lump on the end, sometimes with spikes sticking out. Medieval soldiers would whack their enemies with it.

Groups of Roman soldiers used their big shields to make 4 walls and a roof so nobody could reach them. It was called a 'tortoise' and was a bit like a 2,000-year-old tank!

HA HA! YOU CAN'T GET ME ... OW!

In 1976, a Saxon sword decorated in silver was found by a 9-year-old boy playing in a stream in northern England. It had been lost for over 1,000 years.

Throughout history, armies have used giant catapults to hurl rocks at their enemies. They were really useful for smashing castle walls.

PING!

Revolution

NEXT!

During the French Revolution (1789–1799), King Louis XVI and his wife Marie-Antoinette both had their heads chopped off by a guillotine.

DEFINITELY NOT A KING.

The French Revolution got rid of the king and queen of France, and Napoleon Bonaparte later took over as emperor instead.

In the American Revolution, the USA won freedom from rule by the British on July 4th, 1776. The USA still celebrates Independence Day on July 4th every year.

In 1773, less than 2 years before the American Revolution, protesting Americans climbed aboard 3 British ships in Boston harbour and threw 342 chests of tea into the water. The event became known as the Boston Tea Party.

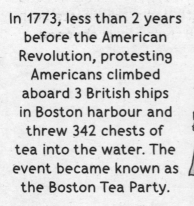

ANYONE FOR TEA?

SPLASH!

TEA

At the start of the Russian Revolution in early 1917, the Russian ruler, Czar Nicholas II, sent soldiers to stop a demonstration. Unfortunately for Nicholas, the soldiers joined the protest.

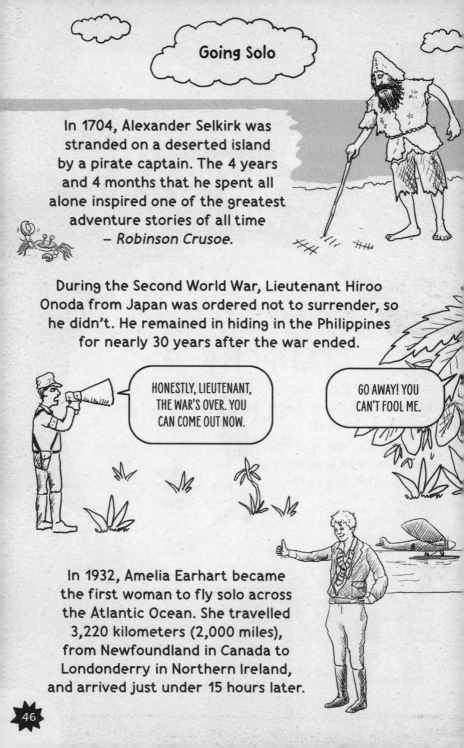

Going Solo

In 1704, Alexander Selkirk was stranded on a deserted island by a pirate captain. The 4 years and 4 months that he spent all alone inspired one of the greatest adventure stories of all time — *Robinson Crusoe*.

During the Second World War, Lieutenant Hiroo Onoda from Japan was ordered not to surrender, so he didn't. He remained in hiding in the Philippines for nearly 30 years after the war ended.

HONESTLY, LIEUTENANT, THE WAR'S OVER. YOU CAN COME OUT NOW.

GO AWAY! YOU CAN'T FOOL ME.

In 1932, Amelia Earhart became the first woman to fly solo across the Atlantic Ocean. She travelled 3,220 kilometers (2,000 miles), from Newfoundland in Canada to Londonderry in Northern Ireland, and arrived just under 15 hours later.

NO SIGN OF LIFE DOWN HERE.

CHAPTER 4: SPACE

Star Types

A red dwarf is a small star that burns at a much lower temperature than our Sun. It is the most common type of star.

A white dwarf is a dead star that is no longer burning.

A supernova is the name given to an exploding star at the end of its life. It's the biggest explosion known to humans.

A red giant is a dying star. The star turns red and grows in size before shrinking into a dead star.

Our Sun is quite a small star. It is classed as a yellow dwarf star.

HOW CAN I BE CALLED SMALL WHEN I'M OVER A MILLION TIMES LARGER THAN THE EARTH?!

Black Holes

ARGH!

A black hole is an area in space where the force of gravity is so immense that nothing, not even light, can escape the hole.

There's a black hole at the centre of the Milky Way, our galaxy (or star system), that is 17 times wider than our Sun.

Because black holes are invisible, we can only find them by looking at how they affect other objects around them.

Our planet will never be destroyed by a black hole as there are none close enough to us.

PHEW! THAT'S ONE LESS THING TO WORRY ABOUT!

Some black holes are as tiny as an atom. Even though they are many times smaller than a grain of sand, they can weigh more than a huge mountain!

Black holes are so powerful that time slows down near them.

GULP!

Our solar system is made up of the Sun and everything that moves around it. If our solar system was the size of an American football field, the Sun would be a small coin ... and Earth would be a grain of sand.

If an 8-year-old child left Earth in a passenger plane, they would be over 1,700 years old by the time they arrived at the edge of the solar system.

ARE WE NEARLY THERE YET?

Space is so big, distances are measured in 'light-years'. A light-year is how far light travels in 1 year.

Light travels so fast that it would go round the Earth about 450 times in 1 minute.

The nearest star is so far away, its light takes over 4 years to reach Earth. That means when people look at the star, they are seeing what it looked like more than 4 years ago.

The furthest star we can see without a telescope is over 16,000 light-years away. When the light left it, Earth was in the Stone Age and woolly mammoths roamed the planet.

Space Walking

Spacesuits allow astronauts to breathe in space. They also protect them from extreme temperatures and from small particles flying around.

On spacewalks, astronauts tie themselves to their spacecraft with a long piece of material called a tether. If they didn't, they'd float off into space.

WHEE!

Astronauts wear jet packs when outside their spacecraft. This is in case they float away and need to power their way back to the craft.

Astronauts get used to floating around in space by practising in a massive swimming pool. They even have full-size models of space vehicles under the water.

RIGHT! WHO'S BEEN THROWING SPACECRAFTS INTO THE POOL AGAIN?

When outside the spacecraft, astronauts may have to fix small, complicated parts while wearing thick protective gloves. These special gloves are fitted with heaters to keep their fingers warm.

OOF ... ALMOST GOT IT ...

I WISH I HADN'T EATEN THAT LAST MUFFIN ...

Astronauts leave the spacecraft through a special airtight room with 2 doors. It's called an airlock and stops air from escaping out of the craft.

55

Space Groups

NASA is the USA's space organization. It stands for 'National Aeronautics and Space Administration'.

Russia's space organization is called Roscosmos. Russia calls its space explorers 'cosmonauts', while the USA calls theirs 'astronauts'.

ROSCOSMOS

DON'T BOTHER ME NOW. I'M BUSY LOOKING FOR ALIENS.

Over 100 scientists work at SETI ('Search for Extraterrestrial Intelligence'), where they look for signs of life in the Universe.

No single country owns the International Space Station. Space organizations from the USA, Canada, Russia, Japan and Europe work together to look after it.

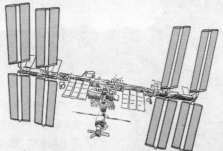

An organization called the Center for Near-Earth Object Studies keeps watch for any dangerous asteroids (space rocks) heading towards Earth.

It's not just Russia and the USA who are space explorers. Astronauts from more than 40 countries have travelled into space. These include Vietnam, China, Brazil, South Korea, Sweden, Mongolia and many, many more.

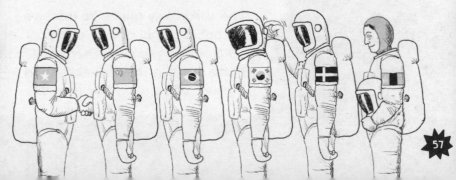

The Milky Way

A galaxy is a huge collection of gas, dust and billions of stars. Our galaxy is called the Milky Way.

Nobody knows exactly how many stars there are in our galaxy, but there are at least 100 billion.

The Milky Way might be massive but it's only one of many billions of galaxies. There are more stars in the Universe than grains of sand on our planet!

The Milky Way, and everything in it, is shooting through space at 2,100,000 kilometres (1,300,000 miles) per hour.

The Sun and the Earth orbit (travel round) the centre of the Milky Way at an amazing 800,000 kilometres (500,000 miles) per hour. Even at that speed, it will take up to 250 million years to make 1 circuit.

HOLD ON!

Space Explorers

The first man in space was a Russian, Yuri Gagarin, in 1961. The first woman was another Russian, Valentina Tereshkova, who was launched on a solo mission 2 years later.

The first man to walk on the Moon was Neil Armstrong in July 1969.

HAPPY BIRTHDAY, DEAR SPACE EXPLORATION! HAPPY BIRTHDAY TO YOU!

Vladimir Titov and Musa Manarov went to space on December 21, 1987, and came back on December 21, 1988. They were the first people to spend an entire year in space.

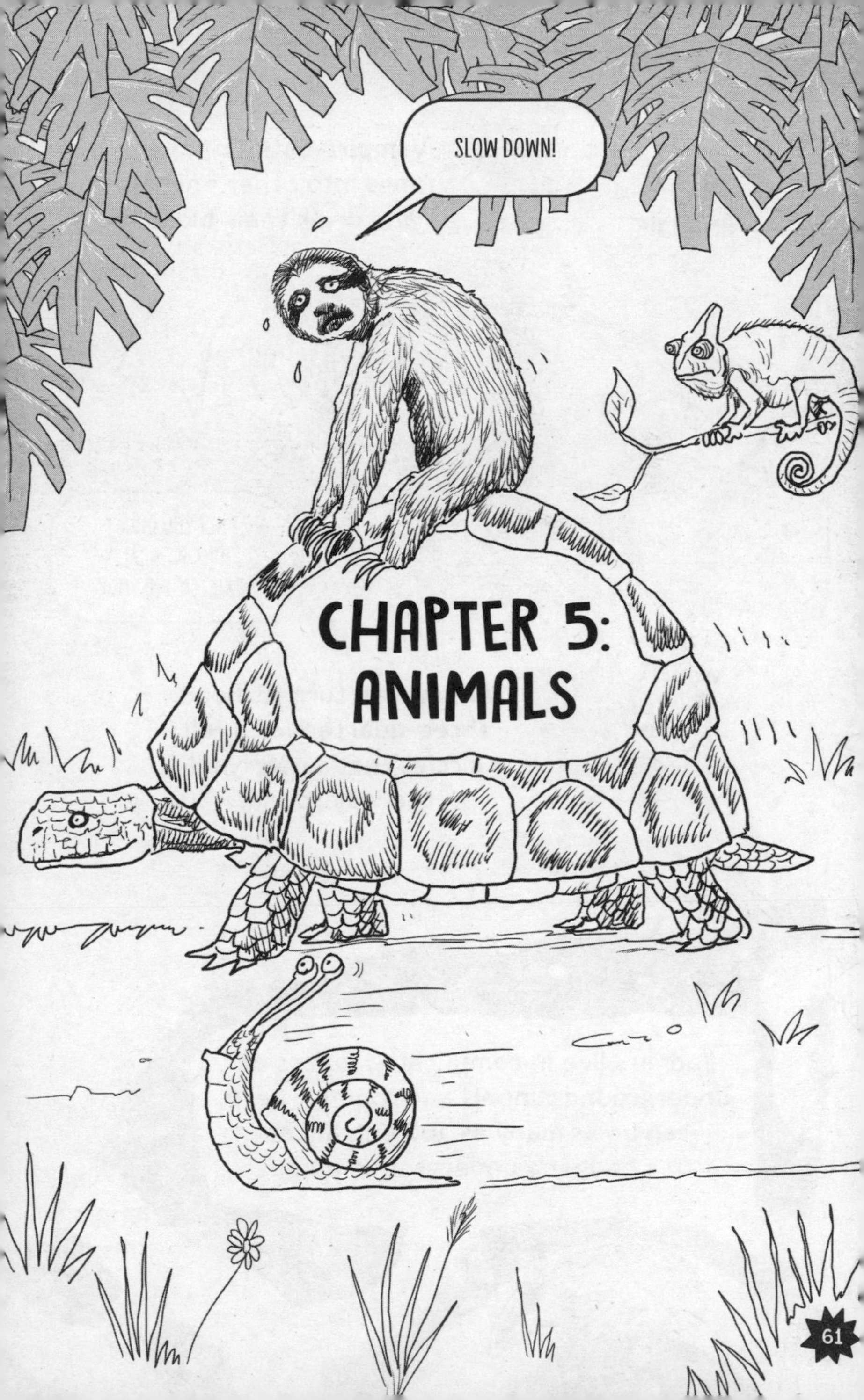

CHAPTER 5: ANIMALS

Night Animals

Vampire bats sink their fangs into other animals and drink their blood.

I BET YOU DIDN'T THINK WE REALLY EXISTED, DID YOU?

An owl can turn its head three-quarters of a full circle. That's nearly all the way round.

Badgers live in complicated mazes of underground tunnels and rooms. There can be as many as 100 entrances to a badger's underground home.

Fireflies are a type of flying beetle. They light up at night and look like tiny flying lights.

Porcupines are covered in sharp, needle-like spikes called quills to protect them from attack. The quills are made out of the same substance as human fingernails.

The Tasmanian devil is about the size of a small dog, has a bad temper, a nasty bite and fills the night with terrifying screeching sounds.

SHHH!

Toxic Animals

RIBBIT!

For centuries, South American tribes have rubbed deadly poison from poison dart frogs on their arrows.

GO ON, TAKE A BITE, I DARE YOU.

Even though a pufferfish contains enough poison to kill 30 adults, they are a very popular meal in Japanese restaurants.

The stonefish looks like a stone. Anyone who accidentally stands on one is in big trouble, because it's the most venomous fish in the sea.

Not only does the female black widow spider have a venomous bite, she also eats the male black widow spider.

WOULD YOU LIKE TO JOIN ME FOR DINNER?

ER ... SORRY. I'M BUSY.

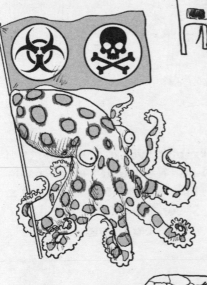

The blue-ringed octopus might look beautiful with its bright blue rings, but this is one of the ocean's most toxic creatures.

HISSS!

A cobra's fangs are hollow so that it can use them to inject venom into its victims.

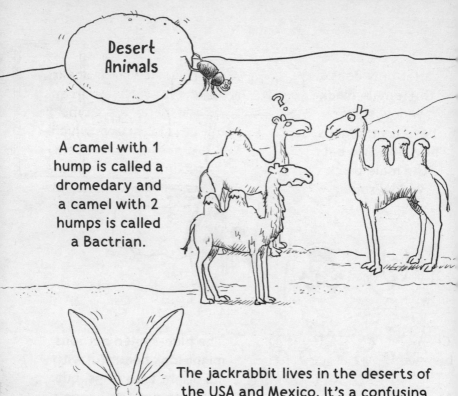

Desert Animals

A camel with 1 hump is called a dromedary and a camel with 2 humps is called a Bactrian.

The jackrabbit lives in the deserts of the USA and Mexico. It's a confusing animal. Firstly, it's not a rabbit, it's a hare. Secondly, it looks like it has borrowed its ears from a donkey!

African meerkats live in groups. One meerkat will always stand on guard duty to watch for predators.

The sidewinder snake moves sideways in an S-shape. It's a type of rattlesnake, which means it can make a rattling sound with the hard, hollow scales at the end of its tail.

Chameleons are famous for being able to change colour. They do this to hide from their predators by blending in with their surroundings.

I'M FED UP OF PLAYING HIDE-AND-SEEK. WE'VE BEEN LOOKING FOR CHARLIE FOR 3 WEEKS.

TE HE HE!

EEK!

Rainforest Animals

Spider monkeys have long, strong tails that they can use as another arm. They can grab things with their tails and even hang from branches with them.

I THINK I NEED A BIGGER TRAP!

Rodents are animals such as mice and rats. The largest rodent in the world is the capybara. It's roughly the size of a large dog.

The green anaconda is the heaviest snake in the world. At up to 250 kilograms (550 pounds), it can weigh as much as 10 eight-year-old children.

The toucan is famous for its enormous colourful beak, which is much, much bigger than its head.

Jaguars look like leopards. They are great hunters and can run at up to 80 kilometres (50 miles) per hour.

The black caiman is the largest of all the alligators. It can grow to 5 metres (over 16 feet). That's 4 eight-year-olds lying head to toe.

WOULD YOU MIND SWAPPING ENDS?

Birds

The Arctic tern spends summer in the Arctic at the top of the Earth and then travels to the Antarctic at the bottom. The return trip is up to 35,000 kilometres (21,750 miles).

HUMM!

Birds have hollow bones. This makes them light so they can fly more easily.

Flamingo couples stay together for life. Lots of other birds do, as well, such as Canada geese, barn owls, puffins and lovebirds.

Coal miners used to take canaries into mines. If the canary fell off its perch, the miners knew there was poison gas around and it was time to leave.

I DIDN'T SIGN UP FOR THIS!

zzzzzz

The wandering albatross' wingspan can be over 3 metres (11 feet) wide, allowing the bird to glide for hours without flapping. It can also fly for months at a time without touching the ground, feeding on octopus, squid and cuttlefish that it plucks out of the sea.

CR-CRACK!

The ostrich is the biggest bird in the world. One of its eggs weighs about the same as 24 chicken eggs.

HURRY UP AND EAT YOUR BOILED EGG. IT'S TIME FOR SCHOOL.

A polar bear's skin is black!

JUST A BIT OFF THE BACK, PLEASE.

Arctic foxes live within the Arctic Circle. Their thick fur, which turns white in winter, helps to keep them warm.

Narwhals are often called 'unicorns of the sea' because of their long, spiralled tusks. A narwhal's tusk can grow up to 3 metres (10 feet) long and is actually an extremely large, pointy tooth.

A reindeer's eyes are golden in the summer and blue in the winter.

A walrus has 2 long tusks. It uses its tusks to get out of the water by sticking them in the ground and dragging itself out.

I DON'T KNOW WHY THEY CAN'T JUST BUILD SOME STAIRS.

The Arctic-dwelling beluga whale can dive for up to 25 minutes, reaching a depth of up to 800 metres (2,625 feet). It can also swim backwards!

Rodents

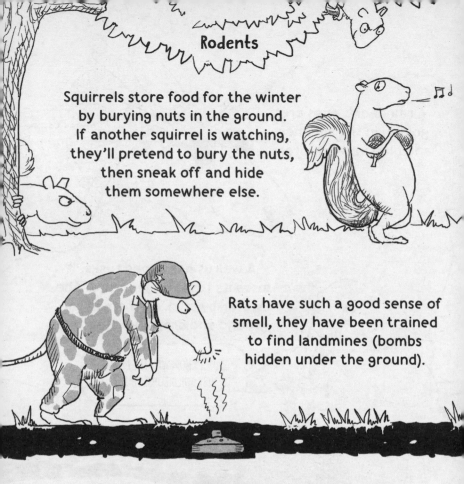

Squirrels store food for the winter by burying nuts in the ground. If another squirrel is watching, they'll pretend to bury the nuts, then sneak off and hide them somewhere else.

Rats have such a good sense of smell, they have been trained to find landmines (bombs hidden under the ground).

A mouse can have 8 babies at the same time. Just 6 weeks later, each of those 8 mice can have 8 babies. That makes 64 babies. Another 6 weeks later, those 64 babies can each have 8 babies. That's 512 new mice in just 12 weeks.

CHAPTER 6:
SPORTS

Olympic Games

The first recorded Olympic Games were held nearly 3,000 years ago in ancient Greece. Chariot racing later became one of the sports.

ER, I THINK YOU'VE GOT THE WRONG YEAR.

Both the Summer Olympics and the Winter Olympics are held every 4 years. The Winter Games and the Summer Games are 2 years apart.

In ancient Greece, every Olympic athlete competed in the nude!

OOPS!

GREAT VIEW FROM UP HERE!

There have been some strange competitions at the Olympics, including obstacle-course swimming, hot-air ballooning and sculpture!

Japanese skateboarder Momiji Nishiya won an Olympic gold medal when she was just 13 years old.

The Olympic flame is lit in Greece and carried by runners to wherever the Games are being held – sometimes on the other side of the world.

The World Cup

The FIFA World Cup is incredibly popular. More than half the world's population watches it on TV.

GO, TEAM!

YAY!

Pelé was the most famous World Cup player ever. He won 3 times playing for Brazil.

WHO'S A CLEVER BOY, THEN?

The World Cup trophy went missing before the 1966 competition. It was found a week later by Pickles the dog. He was awarded a medal for finding it.

NICE WEATHER WE'RE HAVING.

The first World Cup was played in Uruguay in 1930. Uruguay won!

The USA won the first women's World Cup and 4 of the first 9 World Cup events, yet the men's team has never won.

DOINK!

OOF!

POW!

In 2011, Japan's women's team became the first-ever Asian side to win the World Cup.

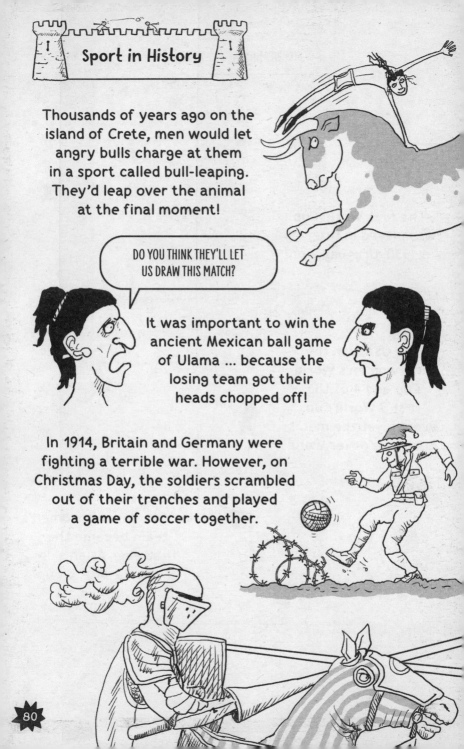

Sport in History

Thousands of years ago on the island of Crete, men would let angry bulls charge at them in a sport called bull-leaping. They'd leap over the animal at the final moment!

DO YOU THINK THEY'LL LET US DRAW THIS MATCH?

It was important to win the ancient Mexican ball game of Ulama ... because the losing team got their heads chopped off!

In 1914, Britain and Germany were fighting a terrible war. However, on Christmas Day, the soldiers scrambled out of their trenches and played a game of soccer together.

Soccer was different in medieval times. Two villages would take part, with hundreds on each team. Whoever brought the ball back to their own village won the game.

In Norway, there's a 5,000-year-old rock carving of someone skiing!

In jousting, 2 knights would charge at each other and try to knock their opponent off their horse. King Henry VIII of England loved the sport, despite all the injuries.

Ready! Steady! Go!

In the Tour de France, cyclists furiously pedal over 3,200 kilometres (2,000 miles) across huge mountain ranges over 3 weeks.

The world's best speed walkers can walk 1.6 kilometres (1 mile) in just over 5.5 minutes. That's faster than most people can run.

The space inside a Formula 1 racing car is so tight that the driver has to remove the steering wheel to get in or out.

PEE-EW!

Swimmers go faster underwater than on the water's surface. They also sweat when they're racing.

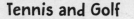

Tennis rules used to state that in the final set, players had to win by 2 clear games. One match lasted over 11 hours! The final score was 70 games to 68.

> I'M NEVER, EVER, EVER PLAYING TENNIS AGAIN!

A player who, in a single year, wins all 4 major tennis tournaments – the Australian Open, French Open, Wimbledon (in England) and the US Open – has won the Grand Slam.

Tennis racket strings are made from cow gut, nylon and similar materials. They also used to be made from sheep gut.

GULP!

84

HOLE IN ONE!

Golf is the only sport to have been played on the Moon. Astronaut Alan Shepard hit 2 balls – the first landed in a crater!

Golf balls have over 300 little dimples on them to help them fly further and straighter.

HE HE!

Golf was invented in Scotland. It became so popular the king banned it because people preferred playing golf to doing military training.

Swimming is one of 5 sports
in the modern pentathlon,
along with fencing, shooting,
horseriding and running.
These were regarded as
the 5 skills a battlefield
messenger needed.

Synchronized swimmers all
move together. To do this,
they use special underwater
speakers to hear the music
they are moving to.

Rowers use a lot of muscles but
it is their legs, not their arms, that
provide most of the rowing power.

Ice hockey is fast. Skaters zoom around at up to 40 kilometres (25 miles) per hour. That's about the same speed that a car drives through town.

The 'skeleton' is extreme sledging, where the rider's face is very close to the ice. The sledge shoots downhill at 130 kilometres (81 miles) per hour with no brakes and no steering wheel.

I THINK I'M GOING TO BE SICK.

Figure skaters can spin up to 300 times in a minute.

Swimmer Trischa Zorn has won 55 Paralympic medals, including 41 golds. Being born blind certainly didn't stop this amazing athlete.

Norwegian skier Ragnhild Myklebust is a real star of the Winter Paralympics. She won 16 golds in cross-country skiing and 27 medals in total. As a result of polio, she skied sitting down.

In 2012, Matt Stutzman won a silver medal for archery despite having no arms. He holds the bow with his foot.

CHAPTER 7:
TECHNOLOGY

Electricity

Electricity was discovered over 2,500 years ago. An ancient Greek noticed feathers and other light objects stuck to a piece of amber after he rubbed it with a cloth.

WOW! GREAT DISCOVERY! ER ... WHAT DO WE USE IT FOR?

Although electricity is all around us, it was Michael Faraday who learned how to create it. In the 19th century, he invented the electric generator to make an electric current.

Some light bulbs turn nearly all of their electricity into heat and only a little bit into light. That's why you can burn yourself touching a lit light bulb.

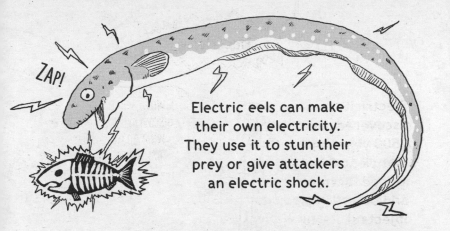

Electric eels can make their own electricity. They use it to stun their prey or give attackers an electric shock.

People think electric cars are very modern, but they were actually invented in 1832. In 1900, 1 in 3 cars in the USA was electric.

WE HAD ELECTRIC CARS BEFORE IT WAS COOL.

Generators make electricity by spinning wires next to magnets. A generator can be powered by wind turning huge wind turbines, water running downhill or by steam from a coal fire.

ZAP!

Inventors

Johannes Gutenberg invented the printing press in the 15th century. Before printing, books had to be copied out by hand. Imagine how long that would take!

Alexander Bell invented the telephone in 1876. He was given a middle name as a present on his 11th birthday, so he is better known to history as Alexander Graham Bell.

DAD, NOW I'M 11, CAN I HAVE A MIDDLE NAME, PLEASE?

Scotsman John Logie Baird invented the first working television. He called it the Televisor.

Inventors apply for 'patents' for their inventions to stop anyone else copying their ideas. Thomas Edison had over 1,000 patents! His inventions include the phonograph (an early music player) and the first usable electric light bulb.

Two French brothers, the Lumières, invented the movie. Their first film was made in 1895 and called *Workers Leaving the Lumière Factory*. It lasted less than a minute.

The first passenger-carrying train was called the 'Puffing Devil'. The inventor, Richard Trevithick, took it for its first trip on Christmas Eve, 1801.

Fantastic Phones

The first mobile phones that people could buy arrived in 1983. They cost about £2,650 ($3,995). That's equivalent to over £7,500 (over $11,400) in today's money.

SORRY! I CAN'T TALK NOW. I'M TOO BUSY WORKING TO PAY FOR MY PHONE.

The first mobile phone call was made in 1973, when the inventor called his rival to brag about his invention.

Modern smartphones use Bluetooth technology to join up with other devices. It's named after a Danish king, Harald 'Bluetooth' Gormsson, who also became King of Norway over 1,000 years ago.

A 17-year-old boy became the world's fastest texter when he took only 17 seconds to text: "The razor-toothed piranhas of the genera Serrasalmus and Pygocentrus are the most ferocious freshwater fish in the world. In reality they seldom attack a human."

TAP TAP TAP TAP

A smartphone is about 100,000 times more powerful than the computer used on the Apollo 11 mission. Apollo 11 was the first mission to successfully land humans on the Moon.

About 1 in 3 phones in the UK get broken and about 1 in 7 are stolen.

OH!

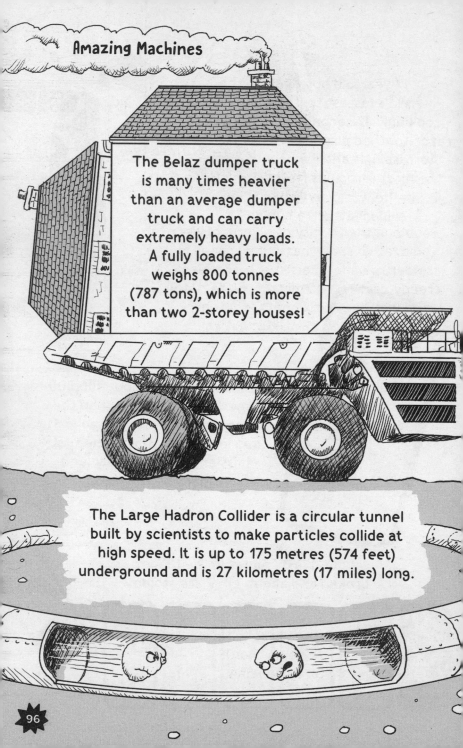

The Belaz dumper truck is many times heavier than an average dumper truck and can carry extremely heavy loads. A fully loaded truck weighs 800 tonnes (787 tons), which is more than two 2-storey houses!

The Large Hadron Collider is a circular tunnel built by scientists to make particles collide at high speed. It is up to 175 metres (574 feet) underground and is 27 kilometres (17 miles) long.

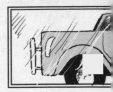

People in the UK city of Liverpool were amazed to see a massive mechanical spider roaming the streets. The giant creepy-crawly — 15 metres (50 feet) tall and weighing 37 tonnes (36.4 tons) — was made as part of a festival.

The Quadski must be the coolest birthday present ever! It's a quad bike that converts into a jet ski, so it can be ridden on land or water.

WHEE!

Vending machines usually sell drinks and snacks. However, in the US, there are 8-storey vending machines that sell cars!

Video Games

Video games have been around for longer than people realize. The first game, *Tennis for Two*, was invented in 1958.

Creating video games can be complicated. In some cases, over 2,000 people might work on developing a single game.

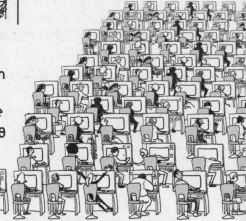

The biggest video games can cost over £100 million (over $120 million) to make. That's enough money to build an entire village with hundreds of houses.

FOR SALE

100,000,000

One of the most popular games ever, *Minecraft*, was created by 1 person in a single weekend. He later sold it to Microsoft for about £1.6 billion ($2.5 billion).

$ TWO BILLION
FIVE HUNDRED MILLION
$ 2,500,000,000.00

Video games are so popular that they make more money than all movies and all music put together.

More adults than children play video games.

DAD ... DO YOU THINK YOU'LL EVER LET ME HAVE A GO?

JUST 5 MORE MINUTES!

Big Building Technology

Japan has a lot of earthquakes.
Tall buildings, such as skyscrapers,
are built on special blocks of
rubber that help them to soak
up all the vibrations.

I'M AFRAID I'M GOING
TO HAVE TO FINE YOU
FOR SPEEDING, SIR.

The Lotte World Tower in South Korea
has 123 floors, but you can reach the
top in just 1 minute. The elevator climbs
past 2 floors practically every second!

Although El Teniente is a mine, its entrance is 2.3 kilometres (1.4 miles) above sea level in South America's Andes Mountains. It has a giant network of over 3,000 kilometres (around 1,900 miles) of passageways.

Using the latest building techniques, a company built a 57-storey skyscraper in China in 19 days.

Atlanta Airport in the USA has over 2,700 arrivals and departures daily. That's more than a flight a minute.

I'VE LOST TRACK!

Healthy Technology

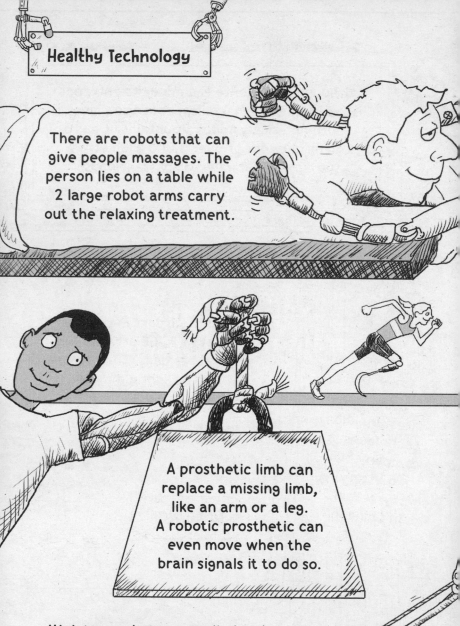

There are robots that can give people massages. The person lies on a table while 2 large robot arms carry out the relaxing treatment.

A prosthetic limb can replace a missing limb, like an arm or a leg. A robotic prosthetic can even move when the brain signals it to do so.

Miniature robots controlled by surgeons can carry out operations on patients.

CHAPTER 8:
UNDERWATER

Sharks

There are over 400 different types of shark.

The great white shark has around 300 sharp, triangular teeth. It can propel itself through the water at speeds of up to 50 kilometres (35 miles) per hour.

Dwarf lantern sharks are no more than 20 centimetres (8 inches) long.

Sharks don't have any bones. Their skeletons are made of cartilage, which is the soft, bendy material that forms your nose.

I WAS HAVING A HORRIBLE NIGHTMARE ABOUT HUMANS!

People think sharks are dangerous, but they only kill about 10 people a year. People kill about 100 million sharks. We're more dangerous by far!

Sharks don't just see, smell and hear their prey. They have an extra sense that allows them to pick up the electricity every living creature gives off.

Down at the Bottom

Despite being 8,849 metres (29,032 feet) high, Mount Everest isn't actually the world's tallest mountain. Hawaii's Mauna Kea is a whopping 10,211 metres (33,500 feet) high. However, over half of it is under the sea.

Volcanoes on land are the ones we notice, but far more volcanoes erupt under the oceans.

The world's longest mountain range is under the sea. It snakes across the world for over 65,000 kilometres (40,000 miles). That's nearly 7 times more than the Andes, the longest range on land.

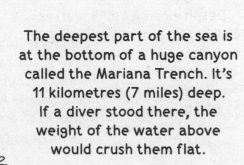

The deepest part of the sea is at the bottom of a huge canyon called the Mariana Trench. It's 11 kilometres (7 miles) deep. If a diver stood there, the weight of the water above would crush them flat.

There are holes on the ocean floor, called vents, that pump out extremely hot liquid. Unique creatures that survive without sunlight make their homes around these vents.

I DON'T SUPPOSE YOU'VE GOT A TORCH, HAVE YOU? I WAS WONDERING WHAT I LOOK LIKE.

Hardly any light goes deeper than 200 metres (650 feet) under the sea. As there is over twice as much sea as land, this means most of the world is always very, very dark.

107

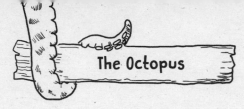

The Octopus

Everyone knows an octopus has 8 tentacles. But not many people know it also has 3 hearts and 9 brains.

I LOVE YOU WITH ALL MY HEARTS!

When an octopus is being chased, it squirts dark ink so its attacker can't find it.

Inky the octopus lived in a tank in a New Zealand aquarium. One night, he climbed out, slid across the floor, squeezed into a pipe, got outside and found freedom in the sea.

An octopus can draw water inside itself and then shoot it back out. The force of the water coming out propels it through the sea.

SEE YA!

You won't find a 7-armed octopus. If an octopus loses a tentacle, it can just grow it back.

Octopuses can change colour to blend in with the background when they want to hide.

109

Sea Mammals

Whales and dolphins don't breathe underwater like fish. They have blowholes on the top of their heads to breathe in air above water.

Whales and dolphins aren't fish. They are mammals, like us, and give birth to babies instead of laying eggs.

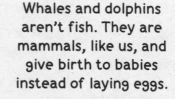

Whales, and especially dolphins, are very intelligent animals. They display problem-solving skills and are thought to feel complex emotions.

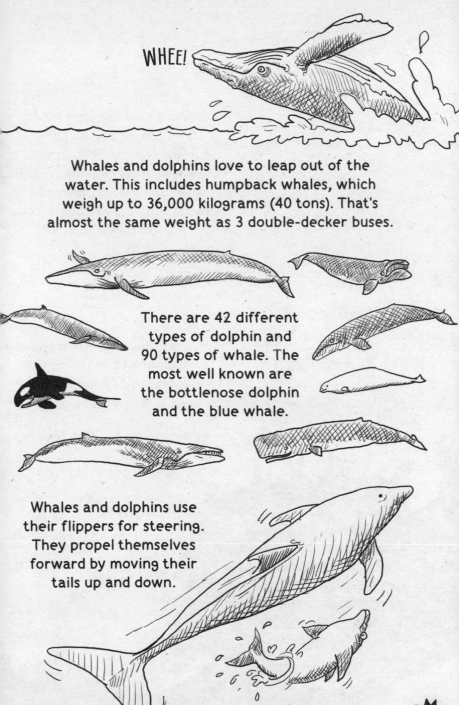

WHEE!

Whales and dolphins love to leap out of the water. This includes humpback whales, which weigh up to 36,000 kilograms (40 tons). That's almost the same weight as 3 double-decker buses.

There are 42 different types of dolphin and 90 types of whale. The most well known are the bottlenose dolphin and the blue whale.

Whales and dolphins use their flippers for steering. They propel themselves forward by moving their tails up and down.

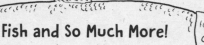

Fish and So Much More!

Coral are tiny sea creatures, some are no bigger than a grain of rice. They come together to form living reefs. Australia's Great Barrier Reef is over 2,300 kilometres (1,400 miles) long.

Crabs have teeth in their stomach to chew up the food they've swallowed.

CHOMP!

MUNCH!

Anglerfish live in the deep, dark ocean. They have a rod on their heads with a light on the end. When smaller fish swim up to the light, they get eaten.

YIKES!

Sea turtles cry. They don't do this because they're sad, though. They cry to get rid of the salt from all the seawater that collects in their eyes and bodies.

BOO-HOO! I'M SO HAPPY SWIMMING AROUND IN THE OCEAN.

One of the world's largest seashells belongs to a type of sea snail. It is nearly 1 metre (3 feet) wide and can weigh up to 18 kilograms (40 pounds).

The eyes of a giant squid are about 25 centimetres (10 inches) wide. That's the same size as a Frisbee.

113

Jellyfish

The box jellyfish is one of the most dangerous animals in the world. Just a tiny amount of venom from its sting can cause a human heart to stop.

GULP!

The lion's mane jellyfish can have 1,200 tentacles, with each one up to 36 metres (120 feet) long. That's as long as 28 eight-year-old children lying head to toe.

Jellyfish don't have hearts or brains. They don't have any ears either.

WHAT ARE YOU THINKING?

NOTHING. I HAVEN'T GOT A BRAIN.

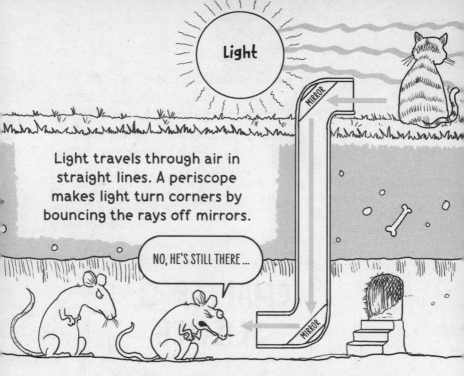

Light

Light travels through air in straight lines. A periscope makes light turn corners by bouncing the rays off mirrors.

NO, HE'S STILL THERE ...

MIRROR

MIRROR

The Sun is about 150 million kilometres (93 million miles) away, but light travels so fast that it only takes the Sun's light 8 minutes and 19 seconds to reach us.

Sometimes light can look like it bends. This happens when it enters water. That's why a straight straw that's halfway in and halfway out of water looks bent.

HOW DOES THAT WORK?

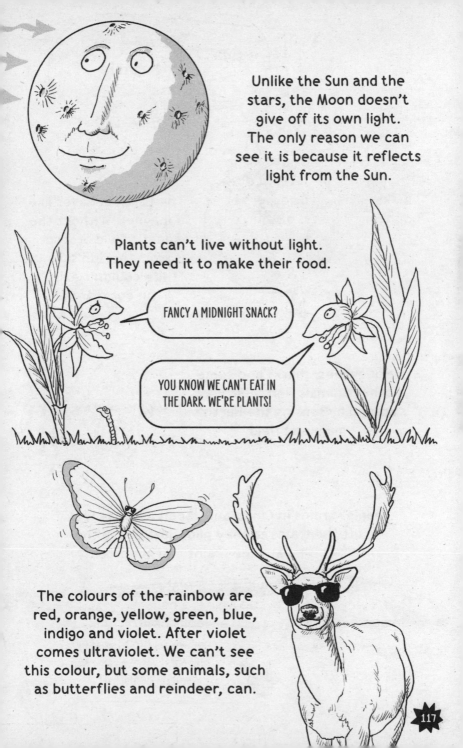

Unlike the Sun and the stars, the Moon doesn't give off its own light. The only reason we can see it is because it reflects light from the Sun.

Plants can't live without light. They need it to make their food.

FANCY A MIDNIGHT SNACK?

YOU KNOW WE CAN'T EAT IN THE DARK. WE'RE PLANTS!

The colours of the rainbow are red, orange, yellow, green, blue, indigo and violet. After violet comes ultraviolet. We can't see this colour, but some animals, such as butterflies and reindeer, can.

Magnets

The Earth behaves like a magnet. Without the magnetic field protecting us from the Sun's winds, life couldn't exist on our planet.

Honeybees, sharks and some other animals find their way around by sensing the Earth's magnetic field.

OMMM!

Maglev trains in China and Japan use magnets to lift the trains so they glide just above the rail. This means the trains can go faster.

SO, EXPLAIN THAT TO ME AGAIN? THE MAGLEV USES A RAIL ... BUT DOESN'T TOUCH IT?

The pull of the world's most powerful magnet is about 2 million times stronger than that of a fridge magnet.

ZAP!

ZIP!

All magnets have a north pole and a south pole. A north pole will stick to a south pole. However, 2 north poles (or 2 south poles) will push each other away.

Iron is magnetic. So are materials with iron in them, such as steel. This means they will stick to a magnet. Nearly every other metal – copper, lead, aluminium and so on – isn't magnetic.

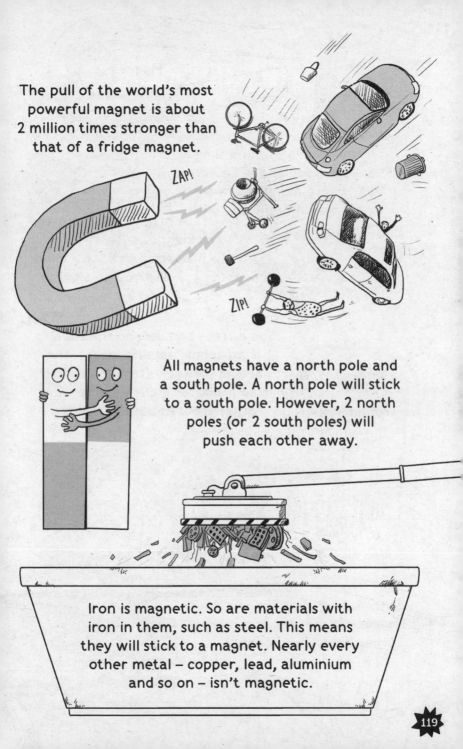

Trees

Trees can live a long time. There's a woodland in California, USA, where many of the trees are over 4,000 years old!

Some trees can defend themselves. If an animal eats its leaves, the acacia tree releases a poison. It also produces a chemical to warn other trees about the danger.

There are over 60,000 species of tree. Brazil has over 9,000 species of tree, which is more than any other country.

GLUG!

SLURP!

Trees drink a lot of water. An oak tree can drink up to 450 litres (100 gallons) of water a day. That's more than 2 bathtubs full.

A tree grows a ring of bark round its trunk each year, so we can tell a tree's age by counting the rings. Trees grow more in years with plenty of sunshine and rain.

Trees produce a lot of the oxygen we need to breathe. They also take in a gas called carbon dioxide. Too much carbon dioxide is bad for the planet.

HMPH! EVERYTHING WE DO FOR YOU AND ALL YOU DO FOR US IS TURN US INTO DESKS AND TABLES.

An opossum can avoid being attacked by falling to the ground and looking dead.

I HOPE HE LEAVES SOON. I THINK I'M GOING TO SNEEZE.

Skunks protect themselves by squirting a smelly liquid at their attackers.

Not all hunters are animals. The Venus flytrap is a plant that catches and eats insects. When an insect lands, the leaves snap shut, trapping the insect inside.

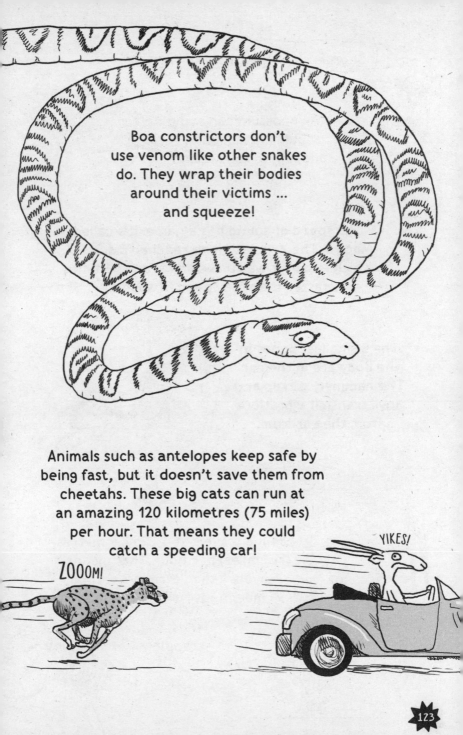

Boa constrictors don't
use venom like other snakes
do. They wrap their bodies
around their victims ...
and squeeze!

Animals such as antelopes keep safe by
being fast, but it doesn't save them from
cheetahs. These big cats can run at
an amazing 120 kilometres (75 miles)
per hour. That means they could
catch a speeding car!

ZOOOM!

YIKES!

Sound

The speed of sound has a name. It's called Mach 1. The X-15 jet plane reached Mach 6.7, which meant it was travelling around 6 times faster than the speed of sound.

The 3 smallest bones in the body are in the ear. The hammer, stirrup and anvil transmit vibrations from the eardrum.

DINNER!

Sound travels at 1,225 kilometres (761 miles) per hour. That means it travels 1 kilometre in 3 seconds (1 mile in just under 5 seconds).

00.03

Sound is caused by waves of air. Without air, there's no sound (unless you're underwater, because water can carry sound as well).

THERE'S A MOVIE CALLED *ECHO* ON LATER. DO YOU WANT TO WATCH IT?

When a sound wave hits a smooth, hard surface, it can bounce back. This is what causes an echo.

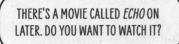

NO. IT'S A REPEAT.

Bats use sound to find their way in the dark. They make high-pitched noises and listen to the echoes to find out what's around them.

Medicine

Vaccines help to stop people getting sick. Smallpox was a horrible disease that had been around for thousands of years, until the smallpox vaccine helped make it disappear from the planet.

Antibiotics are medicines that kill germs. Alexander Fleming won the Nobel Prize for making the first major antibiotic, called penicillin ... and he discovered it by accident.

RUN FOR YOUR LIVES!

Leonid Rogozov became ill during an Antarctic expedition. Luckily, the team had a surgeon called Leonid Rogozov. The poor doctor had to take out his own appendix to save his life.

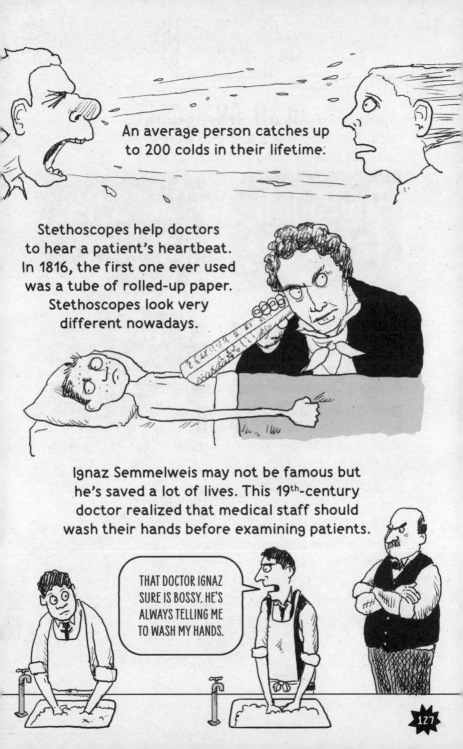

An average person catches up to 200 colds in their lifetime.

Stethoscopes help doctors to hear a patient's heartbeat. In 1816, the first one ever used was a tube of rolled-up paper. Stethoscopes look very different nowadays.

Ignaz Semmelweis may not be famous but he's saved a lot of lives. This 19th-century doctor realized that medical staff should wash their hands before examining patients.

THAT DOCTOR IGNAZ SURE IS BOSSY. HE'S ALWAYS TELLING ME TO WASH MY HANDS.

ALSO AVAILABLE:

ISBN: 978-1-78055-925-4

ISBN: 978-1-78055-926-1